Should you desire to pass this book on to someone else, this space is reserved for your special message to them...

To those wonderful people who understand the significance of making the world a better place than they found it, may your "lessons learned" deepen your resolve to impact lives

Special Thanks To:

Cindy, my lovely wife of thirty-five years, whose persistence and sound advice made *Living Well... Making a Difference* possible and gave me the continued drive to not "give up the ship."

Skippy Kontos, Larry Peterson, Dr. Bill Reynders, Gerry "Wharf Rat" Cook, Fred Human, Bill Marriott, John Hastings, Bill Squires, Garo "Wilson" Mavian and Scott Semko for being the best of friends at critical times in my life.

Mr. Ken Venturi, Secretary of Defense Bill Cohen, and Generals Jim Jones and Jim Mattis: these four men taught me that famous, powerful people can be caring, down-to-earth, and share genuine kindness everywhere they turn. They are men who "get it."

Cindy, Mike Moore, and my sons, Matt and Brad, for your time and insights with the tedious and time-consuming editing process.

Table of Contents

Preface

Thank you for taking some of your precious time to read my second book. As of the beginning of this writing, I am only weeks away from publishing *Living Well…Making a Difference*. The first *Living Well* took about twenty-eight months from inception to print so I thought I would get a jump on this one. I think you also live well by learning from your past and teaching others some of your *Lessons Learned*.

The cover of this book is a picture that my son Matt took of his wife, Stephanie, walking with my grandson Brady in Heber Springs, Arkansas, in 2010. I think it beautifully captures the message of this book…a mom passing on her experiences and knowledge to the next generation. My wife, Cindy, came up with this idea. This picture sits on a nightstand in our guest room in St. Johns, Florida. You can "feel" the peace in this picture.

In the navy, we often came back from missions or training exercises and discussed lessons learned. America calls them "best practices." We learn from the past and make the future better.

My last book, which you may have read, was simply a written version of the inspirational speech I had done for the sailors with whom I had the honor to serve. As the publishing process unfolded, thoughts of new chapters and subjects popped up in this aging mind of mine…and usually while I was in pain during a jog. In addition, audience members suggested several ideas during recent talks.

I have had many people tell me you cannot look back. Well, I am going to…and hopefully for your benefit. I will give you my thoughts, more stories I have heard, and great books I have read that hopefully all fit together and make some sense. Who knows where you're at on this crazy, cosmic ride and what lessons learned you can share with folks before you depart?

Hopefully this book will make an impact on your life so that you will continue to make an impact on others. We still need to remember we are all just a wisp in time…and work on footprints that others will want to follow. Often some of the best experiences are those that hurt the most and taught us the hard way. So why not humble yourself, be transparent, be who you are, and share some of your *Lessons Learned* and *Make a Difference* to others?

As a retired navy pilot fond of checklists, I will leave you with a checklist at the end of each chapter. You can use these as a working list to jot down some of your thoughts as you prepare to leave your footprints for others to follow. Sit back and let's think about life together…again.

Chapter I

"A Lot Of Things Different"

I have learned that if I had a chance to do things again, I would apply some of these lessons learned and have done a lot of things differently.

Some people say, "I would not have changed a thing"… but I think most do not really believe that. There are hearts we have injured and most of us have gotten caught up in materialism, sacrificing special moments of life.

I guess what inspired me to start my second book with this chapter—along with the title—is a song by Kenny Chesney, "A Lot of Things Different." I believe it is his song about lessons learned.

In the song, he sings about how most people say they would do it all the same if they had another crack at life. But he would have done some things differently and so would I. He talks about things like spending more time with his dad while he was alive and going to church when his grandmother said to. He'd spend more time out in the pouring rain and go skinny-dipping with Jenny Carson. He would have said a more meaningful goodbye to a brother headed off to war. The songwriter urges us to recognize special moments in time, understand their significance, and do more with them. I will address this subject more in a future chapter in this book.

Kenny Chesney understands that he should have taken advantage of special moments when he really felt alive. I often tell people at my seminars that you do have an invitation to engage in life and it is called a birth certificate. I am not really sure what people are waiting for… life is what happens while you're planning your future. Those special moments come and go as you are hoping for a future event or possession that you *think* will make you happy, all the while wasting the precious present.

Isn't it funny how we can remember special moments that kind of crystallize in our memory? There are moments that seem trivial at the time but when we look back, we see they had significance and we did not even realize it. We get so caught up in the hectic pace of life that we miss the moment.

Kenny also sings about things we do when we know better, have been warned about consequences, and yet proceed to do them anyway. In his song, he sings that he was warned, "Boy, you're going to wish you hadn't."

How many times in your life have you been told hindsight is twenty-twenty? I know that saying well and still my wife has had to remind me not to look back and punish myself, wounding my spirit. I need to move forward. Some past errors I do need to remember, though, because the pain from my actions was so deep that I never want to go there again. I regret the times when I hurt another human spirit with actions or words or put myself in a position that led to questions of integrity, be they wrong or right. Unfortunately, perception is reality most of the time. I pray that people have forgiven me, as only One of us has ever lived a perfect life.

Had I been given the luxury of hindsight as reality, I would not have to work now. I'm referring to the crystal ball of investing. I love how usually the only person you hear speaking about investments at a cocktail party is the guy who is boasting, "Yeah, I started buying Nike stock before Michael Jordan and Tiger Woods signed with them. Now I'm on easy street." Pride keeps most people from sharing what they have been through, things like what I'm about to share.

I decided to be a land entrepreneur and bought lakefront property in 1985 in the middle of Florida that ended up almost completely drying up. My two acres were now three acres but no longer waterfront. I had been investing in mutual funds since 1983 and in 1987 needed to liquidate some funds to purchase a house in Orange Park, Florida. Everyone said wait until the Dow goes above 3000 in December of 1987 to liquidate. Unfortunately, October 19 of that year saw one of the biggest crashes in market history. I had bought at sixteen dollars a share and liquidated at nine. I'm a buy-high-sell-low kind of guy.

Living Well

In 1991, I had an adjustable rate mortgage around 9.5 percent and for a mere two thousand dollars the bank said they would freeze my interest rate. Interest rates dropped that year; I paid two thousand to have a higher house payment.

In 1995, I bought a house in the Washington, DC, area for $228,000 and sold it four years later for $241,000. Over the next two years, the house almost doubled in value. God did not intend for Andy Andersen to *have money.* I love it when people use that term…what does that mean? Being rich or "having money" is a relative term. I told Cindy one day, "I'm going to tell people at my seminars how much money we have." "You are?" she exclaimed. "Yes, I'm going to tell them *we have enough.*"

But had those investments worked out, I probably wouldn't be where I am now. I enjoy writing and public speaking. Had my investments all worked out and had I not been through what I have been through during the last eleven years since leaving the navy, I wouldn't be here. Maybe I would not have to work or my life would not have crossed the lives I've crossed. I'm not sure I'd have this message or this outlook on life. I might not have grown as much on the inside. I have learned some very painful lessons about life that I can now share from experience and with credibility. This message about what's important could not be better timed for America's Great Recession.

I wish I could remember who said, "When you think your prayers are not answered, just remember that *God gives you what you would have asked for if you knew what He knows.*" I cannot tell you how many times in my life I thought I knew better.

"A Lot Of Things Different"

    So I guess I'm glad I didn't have that crystal ball and life has evolved the way it has. I love the Garth Brooks song "The Dance." In it, he says, "And if I only knew, I could have missed the pain, but then I would have missed the dance. Our lives are better left to chance."

"Growing up happens when you start having things you look back on and wish you could change."

Cassandra Clare, City of Ashes

Living Well

My "Hindsight" Checklist
(List the things that you would have done differently—
items that you can pass on to future generations.)

1. _____

2. _____

3. _____

4. _____

5._____

Chapter II

A Hole In The Roof

I've learned that relationships and things that have eternal impact are far more important than what we see and touch.

Keeping relationships intact and making them a priority is no doubt one of the keys to happiness. One day, a friend and I were having a pretty deep conversation about relationships. He told me a story about a day when he and his son were repairing a leaky roof over his dining room. After they had removed the shingles and tarpaper, they proceeded to pull away the rotted wood that was causing the leak, which left an open hole in the roof. My friend had to run to a quick appointment around lunchtime so his son decided to hit my favorite Scottish restaurant, McDonald's. It was a beautiful, sunny afternoon. Unfortunately, as some of you may know, Florida has a knack for afternoon thunderstorms that can come out of nowhere from the heat and high humidity. Well, as luck would have it, as father and son were taking their breaks, an afternoon storm formed and parked over their house. A heavy downpour ensued. The dining room and living room were flooded.

Needless to say, my friend was not happy and could have easily launched into a tirade at the stupidity and irresponsibility of his son leaving for lunch without covering the hole. But he mentioned that in his studies and countless counseling sessions, he had learned of the importance of relationships in all walks of life, especially family. He felt his relationship with his son was much more important than the water damage from their hole in the roof. The damage to their relationship would leave heart scars, perhaps for life, depending upon the ferocity of the argument and words exchanged. The repairs to the house would take perhaps a week or so and things would be back to normal.

When he told me this story, immediately I thought back to a similar incident in my family when I did not react in the wisdom-filled manner he did.

It was 1995; I was a navy commander and en route to Washington, DC, for another set of orders. We were leaving Orange Park, Florida. My house had been sold and we were just days away from moving. My oldest son, Matt, was helping me clear out the attic above the garage so the movers could box up all our *stuff* collected throughout the years. I told him it was very important to walk on the stringers or ceiling joists because the plasterboard could not support his weight. Next thing I knew, a size thirteen shoe was sticking through the garage ceiling. A hole in the roof!

I was not happy that he had damaged our already sold house. "But, Dad, I just lost my balance!"

I proceeded to berate him and let him know that he was a clumsy oaf and could probably have starred in a scene from *The Three Stooges* show. Here I was, ripping my oldest son out of his senior year in high school to go to a new area in another state for my career, and I was verbally launching into him over a hole in some plasterboard. I was not putting our relationship first; I was more concerned over the expense...wrong priority.

How we treat each other's spirits and souls is so much more critical than the *stuff* that surrounds us and will soon turn to dust. Real happiness and the things we should guard so closely as life unfolds lie in our eternal spirits.

How many times do we vow to win an argument with our spouse over money or some other petty incident? Or let that old "p" word, "pride," get in the middle and wound each other's heart over a hole in the roof? You know, C. S. Lewis once wrote, "Pride is what made Satan the devil."

When our relationships are intact and we are in tune with God, family, and friends, it just doesn't matter what shape our *stuff* is in.

Living Well

I am thankful to my friend for that powerful metaphor for what really matters in life.

"The years run too short and the days too fast. The things you lean on are the things that don't last."

Al Stewart, "Time Passages"

A Hole In The Roof

My Hole-in-the Roof Checklist
(List a few "holes in the roof" in need of repair.)

1. _____

2. _____

3. _____

4. _____

5. _____

Chapter III

When Bad Things Happen

I have learned that when bad things happen, they are almost always accompanied by a significant life lesson. Trials are something everyone will face.

To every audience I speak to, I always mention that I know there are tons of issues in the crowd. Life is tough. The economy, terrorists, oil spills, divorces, etc., etc. Chances are everyone is either coming out of a crisis, in one now, or headed into one. But when I look back at my life, it was during the storms that I learned the most.

Plebe year at the naval academy was a challenging and character-building experience. I would not want to go through it again but it taught me a lot about myself and how to balance priorities under stress.

I also bonded with lifelong friends. Like many academy graduates, I still have nightmares that I am late for formation or have not prepared properly for an exam.

When you go through a crisis with someone, you form some strong bonds. Many say those stressful moments can make a difference in combat.

Speaking of which, as a naval aviator, I had to go through a simulated prisoner-of-war school called SERE (Survival Evasion Resistance Escape). SERE focuses on the possible phases of a downed aviator. Several Vietnam POWs who were subjected to the real thing (only much, much worse, of course) have said that the preparation in SERE school made a big difference in their mental attitude and perseverance. I know I was amazed at what the body can do without food and sleep for several days. The debriefing after SERE was very revealing about deception techniques and the games your mind can play on you.

Besides those tough, planned phases of life, many unplanned, tough events have had an incredible impact on my life. For Cindy and me, the first crisis we faced as a couple was the difficult birth of our oldest son, Matthew. I was in flight training in Pensacola, Florida. The date was July 12, 1978. I was on my sixth flight in familiarization flight training and Cindy went into labor—twenty-four hours of it…lots of pain. I came off the flight schedule and headed to the hospital with my wife. Her labor was not progressing as it should have and the debate was continuing about a possible C-section. As it ended up, the doctor in charge of the department took over because Matt had his umbilical cord wrapped around his neck. After hours of deep pain and heroic effort from Cindy, he was born with what I called a "cone head" because he was in the birth canal so long. I kept asking the nurses if he would ever be normal. Matt is an Annapolis graduate, class of 2001.

Because of the saddle block anesthesia and very difficult labor, an embolism was cut loose in Cindy and lodged in her brain, causing her to have two grand mal seizures. She was transferred by ambulance to Baptist Hospital in Pensacola as my cone-head son was being tended to by the navy hospital staff (twenty-two years later, he would be in Pensacola as a navy pilot in training). In tears, I followed the ambulance in my Toyota Celica wondering what the heck was going on in my life!

Cindy ended up recovering several days later and she and Matt came home from their respective hospitals. But our navy medical insurance did not cover all the hospital bills so we were left with a portion of the bill to pay.

As flight training progresses, eventually you have to put a preference card in to Washington, DC, to request your first duty station or operational squadron. My bills were hefty for a young ensign making twelve thousand dollars a year with a wife and baby at home. I requested Jacksonville, Florida, because of the inexpensive cost of living compared to the other duty stations in California and Hawaii. The needs of the navy were pushing all pilots west at that time. However, I was one of very few to get Jacksonville that year.

Living Well

Not sure my special request had anything to do with it, but it sure was coincidental, and what a blessing Jacksonville has been to us. Out of twenty-four years in the navy, seventeen were spent in this city. Both boys were pretty much raised in Orange Park and we have met lifelong friends. The weather is terrific and the area is beautiful. There are some very nice people in the South. Cindy and I were both raised in Chicago but I decided to retire from the navy here and the blessings keep coming. I find it amazing, the good things that came out of a very traumatic event. I guess God has a plan after all.

In 1991, I was up for orders out of my department head tour in a navy squadron. I had been selected for commanding officer of a squadron and had another set of orders before coming back to Jacksonville. I was up against another navy commander and friend…one of us was staying in Jacksonville as an air wing maintenance officer and another was headed to Naval War College in Newport Rhode Island. I did not want to rip my kids out of school and uproot the family for a year. Neither did my competitor. Well, he won…kind of. We moved to Newport and lived on base in a small eleven-hundred-square-foot government-provided bungalow with two teenage boys.

We did enjoy the beautiful Newport area and met some great people. However, a blessing was coming that we were not aware was in the plan for our life.

Both boys had been begging for a dog for years. Cindy and I resisted because of the inconveniences and knowing we would end up with most of the care, no matter what the kids promised. What we didn't consider was how much the joy in our life would increase through the unconditional love of a pet.

When we finally relented to their wishes, the boys and I looked at several animal rescue shelters throughout Massachusetts but didn't bother looking in Rhode Island. We found a beautiful Dalmatian named Bonnie but decided to look for five more minutes to ensure she was the best choice. When we came back to get her, she was gone…darn the bad luck. There was another plan. The next week, my little voice told me to check Providence, Rhode Island. As we entered the shelter, one dog stood out. Her name was Sandy; she had long, beautiful, blond hair, and was probably a cross between collie and yellow lab. She was full grown and the kids really wanted a puppy. Both Cindy and I could see the quality in Sandy and told the boys we'd take her or nothing as we walked out of the shelter. My oldest son turned to us and said, "I guess we'll take her and call her Dusty."

To this day, I still think that is why we were sent to Newport. I certainly did not tear the place up academically and, so far in my life, that master's degree I earned has had no impact. Dusty had a huge impact. We loved her and she loved us deeply. She was calm, patient, loving, and fun. I would hate to think of my life without Dusty in it for fifteen years.

When we put her down May 18, 2006, it was one of the saddest days of my life. Watching my best friend die in my arms still tears me up. I am so glad that my prayer to stay in Jax was answered with another plan… one far better.

Living Well

"People wish to be settled; only as far as they are unsettled is there any hope for them."

Ralph Waldo Emerson

When Bad Things Happen Checklist
(List the things that seemed terrible at the time, but
ended up being a blessing.)

1. _____

2. _____

3. _____

4. _____

5. _____

Chapter IV

Moments In Time: The Precious Present

I have learned to enjoy the precious present and be in the moment.

Have you ever had a crystallized moment, a moment that just freezes in your mind and has a permanent spot in your memory banks?

I can remember the rock I stood on in our trailer park when I was five years old and first rode my bike without training wheels. The bike was a little red Huffy. That was a moment in time. More moments in time: when I first saw my son Matt being born or when I was radioed about Brad's birth at twenty-seven thousand feet over the Atlantic headed out on a navy mission. I could go on and on. You have hundreds of those moments, too. Somehow your brain or that spirit inside you knows those are lifetime moments.

Those moments are the precious present. What you are living today, right now as you read this book, is also the precious present. But how many times are those moments stained with worry about the future or dreads and guilt about the past? So many times, we ruin the present by living in the past or being anxious over the future. I am speaking to myself here as much as my reader in that I am a terrible second-guesser, always wondering why I didn't optimize the first time. But I have learned so many times that when I look back, I got what was best for me.

We so often ruin the precious present by wanting more. "Boy, I know I should enjoy my kids while they're young…but how am I going to save for their education in this terrible economy?" You only have eighteen summers with them then, in most cases, they're gone. I wish so badly I could have some of those moments back with my kids…those times are gone now. That's why there is so much joy in a grandchild…something I had heard about but didn't "get" 'til I saw my first grandchild. In a way, grandchildren allow you to relive your time with your kids, time that your heart misses so badly.

So many of our precious present moments are wasted, spent wishing for *more.* "Boy, I'll really be happy after I get promoted, when my kids leave the house, when I lose ten pounds, when I get divorced, when I'm making six figures, when my husband changes, when I'm out of debt," etc., etc…need I go on? Next thing you know, you're out of time. You're on your hospice bed, the blood starts to draw in from your extremities to your chest to protect your vital organs for your last few moments, your breathing becomes rapid and shallow, then there is one last wisp of breath from your mouth and you're gone…it's over: no more precious presents.

No hospice patient I have ever worked with wished they had more *stuff*…just more time. Time to be happy, time to say, "I'm sorry," time to say, "I love you" just once more. They wish for time to listen to a bird sing, feel a cool rain, or watch one more sunset. Precious presents. Every morning when I swing my pain-filled knees out of bed, I thank God for one more day. Tomorrow is not guaranteed.

A great book by Dr. Timothy Miller entitled *How to Want What You Have* has a chapter on the precious present. He brilliantly points out the various ways people waste time in needless pursuits of what they think will bring them happiness.

Dr. Miller states, *"This is* the precious present but strangely, sadly, few people know it." He says that when you are older, you will look back and think, *I was younger then, thinner, had more hair, more sex, healthier, a good job, worried too much, got tired and discouraged at times, but really life was very good…then* (1). Once life's basic needs are met, socioeconomic status is unrelated to happiness (2).

Since this book is about life's lessons that I have learned, I will confess one more thing along these lines.

Living Well

My wife will like this part…this is big for me. My entire life, I have dreamt of living on a fresh-water lake. It has always occupied part of my thinking process and brain capacity. (Some of my friends think this is dangerous since my brain space is at such a premium.) Anyhow, I had always hoped to own a lakefront home. Well, I now realize, at age fifty-seven, with my financial history (buy high, sell low), current economic great recession, and rough post-navy career…it ain't gonna happen. I've learned to be content with my twenty-five-hundred-square-foot house in St. Johns, Florida, on a little fresh-water pond! I refuse to waste any more heartbeats and precious presents hoping for something that won't add any more joy to my life. Having researched and written two books now, I found that all studies, interviews, and people confirm what I already suspected: more *stuff* does not bring you joy.

I hope this chapter keeps you from wishing for more when more truly does not add life to your years. Enjoy each precious moment because, for the time, that's really all you have. You just never know when you will slip into eternity.

"The butterfly counts not months but moments, and has time enough."

Rabindranath Tagore

Moments In Time: The Precious Present

My Precious Presents Checklist
(List some precious presents you wish you had back.)

1. _____

2. _____

3. _____

4. _____

5. _____

Chapter V

Going With The Flow

I have learned to take what life gives me in stride and know that it has a reason.

Now, some of you may think this may be about my biological need to head to the "facilities" more often as I age…but it is not. As I write this, it is in the brutal winter of 2010, Valentine's Day. Cindy and I just attended a movie and we saw a preview of a movie coming out this spring…but, sorry, can't remember the title. The movie stars Ben Stiller and is about a guy being comfortable with no direction in life. He basically was doing nothing but was comfortable with that…just going with the flow. I love a quote by one of the characters in the preview, which was something like, "I'm finally embracing the life I was given." I can identify with that quote because that is me.

Living Well

I am going to share a very personal struggle that I am now comfortable with…but I know is also an issue with most people on this earth. I am on my seventh job in eleven years since having left the navy. I thought by now that I would have my corner corporate office downtown and be driving my 5-series BMW. But that wasn't in God's plan for me. I remember when a "head hunter" gave me a profile test and said, "Andy, you just don't fit the corporate mold." He said the results of the profile test indicated I should be a preacher, teacher, social worker, doctor, etc. In other words, my Meyers Briggs test had me pegged as someone who has to visibly impact people's lives.

But a writer and public speaker? As they say on the Monday night football pre-game show, "C'mon, man!" Fifteen years ago, I was petrified of public speaking. I almost did not get into the naval academy because my ACT English score was only 19 with a 33 in math! This makes no sense…but the events of the last thirteen years have brought me to a place I thought I would never be. You want to see God laugh? Tell Him the plan for your life.

In 1997, I suffered my first professional setback, having achieved everything I wanted throughout my naval career. I did not get selected to command an air wing. I took it hard as all the ducks were lined up but it didn't happen. The guys who did get selected were good leaders and well deserving of the positions. But I'll admit it was a hard pill to swallow and some of you reading this can understand where I am coming from. Did I deserve a chance to command an air wing?

Maybe not, but as I look back upon it now, what *did happen* was all part of a bigger plan to exercise my passion of trying to improve others' brief time on earth. I am now doing what I never would have guessed.

Instead of an air wing, I was sent to supposedly the largest squadron in the navy, VP-30, the P-3 training squadron with over twelve hundred staff and students to impact. I started a motivational seminar for the troops about adding meaning to your life. This was an add-on to the financial lecture I had started six years earlier about living within your means and how devastating poor finances can be on your family and professional life. That seminar refuses to die. I have been pushed by wonderful people along this path into a website, my first book, this book, and a "Road Rage Diffuser" thank-you paddle for your car. Cindy and I have started a small business to offer this simple message to corporate America about maximizing your heartbeats and impacting lives. Having been downsized, gone out of business, lost contracts, and had corrupt leaders...I've seen it all. Enduring this extremely painful and humiliating path has led me to doing what I love most, which is speaking to people about what really matters. I have been in the arena and have battle scars to discuss. The level of pain and the number of people who have been through similar experiences amazes me. So many people need healing, especially in this great country now. Nothing excites me more than knowing that something I say during one of my talks might change the life of one person sitting in the audience, in deep pain but suffering silently.

Living Well

The business we started is just sustaining now, making enough to cover costs and support my favorite local charities. Because Cindy and I have lived within our means, and with my navy pension, I can continue to pursue this dream and what I was meant to do. It just took a while to get it through my hard head.

I personally struggle with taking all aspects of life as they come instead of having to maximize everything! Barry Schwartz wrote a great book called *The Paradox of Choice: Why more is less*. He talks about how some people have to maximize everything instead of being content with what life gives them (1). We are choice-aholics in America. We have so many consumer options making us feel we need to get the very best. And if we don't, we think we haven't maximized our happiness and time on earth. This philosophy leads to added stress in trying to research and maximize our choice. This is one of the areas I struggle with quite a bit. I've had people tell me I have ADD (attention deficit disorder) but a psychologist friend thinks I also have OCD (obsessive compulsive disorder) from my regimented, compulsive life of discipline as a navy pilot. Hmmm...interesting...I have to double-check and make sure all the checklists are done and everything is neat and orderly. Yet I can walk through the house, see several things I've forgotten to do, and go from one project to the next, never having finished any of them (some of you can relate). This reminds me of a line from one of my favorite comedians, Stephen Wright: "For my birthday I got a humidifier and a dehumidifier...put 'em in the same room and let 'em fight it out."

Going With The Flow

So I continue to work on this, realizing that in America, we are blessed with so much. True happiness is not found in stuff but in people and relationships. You and I still have time left. We have time to interact with our loved ones, our friends, and the hurting strangers in our sphere of influence. That's where true joy comes from and the inner peace for which we all strive. We don't need to maximize our stuff or do something with our life that society says is success. Each of us can just make a difference with the hand we were dealt...it is a built-in need.

This concept is beautifully depicted in my favorite movie, *It's a Wonderful Life.* In the film, George Bailey is going to take his own life because his small building-and-loan company is facing failure due to Uncle Billy losing an eight-thousand-dollar deposit. George feels he has failed when he compares himself with his brother, the war hero, and his friend Sam Wainwright, the successful millionaire. Staying in his hometown, raising a family, and running the family business was not the vision he had for his life.

I once had dinner with a good friend, Dr. Tim Schneider, a prominent Jacksonville ophthalmologist. I love how he explained what George was dealing with: simply accepting *the gap.* There is a gap between where he was in life and where he *thought* he should be. George Bailey is not the only person having trouble accepting the gap. Many men and women today face the same issue. This might help explain why the suicide rate is so high. It's great to have dreams because they provide hope. However, many will not attain utopia as they *think* it should be. So accept your gap if you have one. Perhaps you have already and are at peace.

Go with the flow, my friend, and enjoy your time on this beautiful earth because it truly is a wonderful life.

"Thank God for unanswered prayers."

Garth Brooks

My "Going with the Flow" Checklist
(In what areas of your life do
you need to go with the flow?)

1. _____

2. _____

3. _____

4. _____

5. _____

Chapter VI

Slowing Down

I have learned that the more I slow my life down, the more I feel at peace.

I must confess I drive about five to ten miles over the speed limit. My schedule is jam-packed and I try to maximize my time, despite what I learned from Barry Schwartz about doing the exact opposite in *The Paradox of Choice: Why more is less.* He points out that we often sacrifice precious time and satisfaction by being unhappy with what we have.

My wife, Cindy, is constantly telling me to slow down. This break-neck pace we live is just feeding on itself and I don't see any turning back. I did an entire chapter on driving in *Living Well...Making a Difference* because I believe the way we drive is representative of where society is *headed*. We act like it's all about "me"; I'm not going to let you merge, my time is more important than your time…get out of *my* way. My friends who are police officers say they are looking for you at about twelve miles over the speed limit. Evidently, people make more money than I do because tickets are expensive and your insurance rates go up. I thought it was just men that speed, but I'm finding it's just as many women…and some with blue hair!

This fast pace is literally killing people. A woman in a hurry cut another woman off on the Buckman Bridge in Jacksonville a few months back, sending her SUV into the St. Johns River and the poor lady into eternity. Another man in a hurry on his way home from the grocery store cut off a woman on north I-95, killing her and her kids. Another man on one of those racing motorcycles came up so fast behind a woman she swerved to get out of the way, killing herself and some passengers. *We are not getting it.*

In Phil Callaway's book *Making Life Rich Without Any Money,* he says we don't need anyone to make more megabytes for our computers, or speed up our cell phones or microwaves. We need someone who can slow things down and ease the stress, pain, and crazy, break-neck pace that literally saps the life out of us. The technology industry basically feeds off the "quicker is better" philosophy, so that you will upgrade. They entice you to keep up with the Joneses and stay in debt at approximately 22 percent APR, making your minimum payment. The manufacturers have most of this technology laid out and ready for future consumers who still will not have learned their lessons from our great recession.

My problem is I don't know how to say no. Like Ray Barone in the sitcom *Everyone Loves Raymond,* I do not want to disappoint anyone. I have this passion to impact lives but it often runs my battery low. If we get run-down, it impacts others and we sap other spirits.

Early in his ministry, Jesus was very popular and was doing great things for people with miracles and teachings. The Apostles said (and I am paraphrasing), "Hey, you are really popular right now; you've got to go here and there." Jesus replied, "No, I need to go out into the peace of the wilderness to pray and rest."

This fast pace also causes us to miss the precious moments in time. Oh, how I wish I had not wasted some of that time with my kids. I cannot get it back. Rushing through a naval career often focused on the wrong *stuff.* I used to think life would be really great when my kids were out of diapers. Then it would be great when they weren't *sticky* anymore. It would really be great when they weren't smart-aleck teenagers. Won't it be nice when they are out of college and we are out of debt? Well, we are almost there. Our mortgage is small, we have no consumer debt, and our kids are adults with their own mortgages. Now Cindy and I sit on the front porch swing, look at photo albums, and dream of *the good old days.*

It also stresses me out when I am running late, weaving in and out of traffic to make appointments, snapping at my wife, losing things, etc., etc. Amazing how much nicer life is when you build some slop time into it and have more time for what really counts. Save some time to recharge your batteries.

I think parents are now filling their kids' lives with so much "stuff" in hopes of making their children better future adults. Well, they have to be in ballet, soccer, T-ball, plays at school, church youth groups, Boy Scouts, etc. These are all fine things, but how many times a week do you sit down for a family meal, look each other in the eye, and really *listen* to what is going on in your kids' lives? I think too much stuff is not good when it starts to cut in on quality time with family and friends. The impact moms and dads have on children's development in the home is huge. Some families need to have two incomes just to put food on the table. God bless them. However, both parents working just to have a bigger house and luxury cars and all the stuff to the detriment of what really counts for the kids is not a good thing. I have often struggled with this thinking: if Cindy had just worked more, we would have more of the bigger stuff like some of my contemporaries. But the majority of the time she remained at home, especially when I was on deployment. I think the two fine gentlemen I have as sons is due in large part to my wife and her dedication to them at a critical time in their character development.

The technology boom has been impressive. However, as children's fingers and hand-eye coordination improves with Xbox technology, they are losing critical social skills by not going outside the home and interacting with other children. Social skills are vital to future mental and social stability and life success.

Slowing Down

I used to consider it a punishment to have to come inside. My mom said, "You have to be home by five o'clock to have dinner as a family." I have heard some kids consider it punishment to have to go outside. Wow...when did that change?

Kenneth Greenspan of New York's Presbyterian Hospital once claimed that stress leads to 90 percent of all diseases (1). Stress reduction is becoming a growth industry. I rest my case.

Put the brakes on your life a tad...you and those you love deserve it.

"The increasing speed at which we live is costing us what we value most."

Phil Callaway

My "Slow Down" Checklist
(What are some things you can do
to slow your pace?)

1. _____

2. _____

3. _____

4. _____

5. _____

Chapter VII

From Success To Significance

I have learned that people truly want to lead lives of significance.

I decided to name this chapter after the title subscript of a great book by Bob Buford called *Half Time*. It's all about changing your game plan from success to significance (1).

The theme of Mr. Buford's book is about how people find out that the pursuit of power and *stuff* has a shallow agenda and does not bring the peace and self-satisfaction that they thought it would when they started the climb up the corporate ladder. Now it's time to find meaning and significance, as discussed in Harold Kushner's brilliant work *When All You Ever Wanted Isn't*

Enough. It is through finding a life with meaning that we find true inner peace for our souls (2).

Now that I have been retired from my military career for over eleven years, my fondest memories are of the lives I hopefully impacted in a positive way. As an old sinner full of issues, like anyone else, I'm sure I impacted some lives in a negative way also and that always weighs heavy on my heart…a deep regret. But every once in a while, someone will come up to me and tell me a sea story, as we call it, about how I made a difference in their life. Nothing makes my soul smile deeper.

I retired in Jacksonville, Florida, where they say you can't swing a dead cat without hitting at least a dozen retired captains. During one of three unemployment periods in my post-military life, I once had a local head hunter tell me there was nothing he could do for me because, "You retired captains are a dime a dozen." His comments deeply hurt as I was facing my second unemployment period with one son in college and, according to this guy, not much hope for a dime-a-dozen military retiree.

As I age and talk to those aging with me, I am finding that people want to be engaged in something that has meaning. Jim Cardosi, a friend and fellow naval officer who served with me in several navy jobs, had this concept capture his heart. Tragically, his wife, Cindy, died of a form of frontal lobe dementia at age fifty-one. After her passing, Captain Cardosi had several good offers for employment but looked at me one day and said, "I have to do something now that is as meaningful as caring for my dying wife was." His priorities about what really matters had changed. I thought that was very powerful. It was a crystallized moment in my life. Jim is now entering the priesthood as a widower and ready to affect lives and prepare them for eternity.

Bill Squires, another good friend, has had a very successful sports management career. As many before him, he has felt a calling for a life-giving cause. Bill has worked for George Steinbrenner in running Yankee Stadium, was in charge of stadium operations for the New York Giants and the Cleveland Browns, and was one of the driving forces in the opening of Disney's Wild World of Sports in Orlando. Unfortunately, Bill's son Sean, a wonderful young man, has cystic fibrosis. Bill's focus and passion now is raising money to find a cure for this difficult disease and he has been recognized as running one of the most successful charity campaigns in US history. I love what I just heard my friend say in our last phone call: "Failure is not an option." Perhaps you'll catch Sean's smiling face on the side of their CF campaign truck.

Admiral Scott Semko is another close friend who has also noticed the same phenomenon. The more people he talks to, the more he hears they want to do something with meaning. He now mentors leadership seminars at the University of North Florida for America's future leaders. We talk about how this need to make a difference is growing as baby boomers approach retirement.

Living Well

The most powerful testimony to this desire in people's lives is what I often hear in the last few words of those dying in hospice. So many people want to know if their time on this earth had significance: did their life mean something? Again I reference Harold Kushner's book *When All You've Ever Wanted Isn't Enough*. He talks about how human happiness has three basic components. One is physical: a roof, water, food, air, etc. Then the psychological needs of acceptance and self-worth. The third is the deep spiritual and soul need: what is life really all about, why am I here, and will my life mean anything? (3) The pursuit of the first need by America and the world, getting more *stuff*, driven by greed, has caused much of our financial collapse. Sadly, in pursuit of the first, people neglect the last two needs, which are the very ones that lead to contentment and inner peace.

As I now see it, the beauty of aging is discovering what really matters in life. I am reading a book by Max Lucado titled *Outlive Your Life: You were made to make a difference*. This book is all about this concept. Lucado reminds us that we didn't ask to be born. The situation we are in is all we get. We only have one shot at it... so we need to make it count and give it our very best. That is what we were made to do (4).

"Don't strive to be a person of success...but a person of value."

Einstein

My Success-to-Significance Checklist
(Things that will help you outlive your life.)

1. _____

2. _____

3. _____

4. _____

5. _____

Chapter VIII

Holes In The Fence

I've learned that just as holes left by nails in a fence will always be there, so will your words that leave scars on people's hearts.

When I do my seminars, I have a part where I stand in the middle of the crowd and say, "This acne-scarred, arthritic right hip, planter's fasciitis left foot, fifty-seven-year-old body of mine is dying," a state of biological shutdown. Some of us are further along in that process than others. This piece of protoplasm's function is to provide a transportation vehicle to get my spirit to your spirit to interact and make an emotional deposit or withdrawal. When our spirits are in tune and producing harmony, people are happy and at peace.

Living Well

I heard Dr. David Jeremiah give a talk one day on television and he spoke of a boy who was having trouble controlling his anger. His father said, "Every time you get mad at someone, I want you to go and just pound the heck out of a nail into the fence in our backyard." The next day, little Jimmy said, "Dad, I got mad at Johnny today." Dad said, "Okay, son, go in the backyard and pound a nail in the fence to release your anger." Next day, "Dad, I got mad at Bobby today." Dad commented, "Alright, son, go pound another nail." The next day it was Brad. Then one day little Jimmy told his dad that he did not get mad at anyone today. His dad replied, "That's terrific, son…how about going out to the fence and removing one nail?" The next day little Jimmy again did not get angry with anyone and Dad had him pull another nail. About a month later, little Jimmy had his anger under control and all the nails in the fence had been removed. Then Jimmy's dad did something profound. He took Jimmy in the backyard and said, "I want to show you something." He took Jimmy's fingers and made him feel the holes in the fence. Dad said, "Those holes left by your nails will always be there. Those holes represent scars left on people's hearts by your angry words."

In *Living Well…Making a Difference*, I discussed the absurdity of the saying, "Sticks and stones may break my bones but words will never hurt me." Words are an extremely damaging weapon that wound people's souls. I think what makes them so damaging is it is one person's spirit damaging another spirit. As the late Stephen Covey once said, "We are not human beings with an occasional spiritual experience; we are spiritual beings in a human experience."

This again points to the studies that confirm people are happier when relationships are in tune, no matter how much *stuff* they have. Life is about interacting and caring about each other—something that is quickly eroding as computer games, long-range social networking, and road rage continue to grow.

One of the biggest lessons I have learned is just how powerful the words are that emerge from my mouth. It is critical that I engage my brain before my mouth. Damaging words were said to me during my childhood that I still remember to this day.

I grew up with a bad case of acne. It was extremely humiliating and painful, especially for a teenager who was trying to fit in and be accepted. One of the forty-five-year-old quotes I remember to this day is, "If I looked like that, I wouldn't even go outside." My squad leader at the naval academy during plebe summer walked up to me in formation and said, "Andersen, you've got to do something about your face." My entire platoon heard him say that. I wanted to hide under a brick in Tecumseh Court.

Each of us, including the big, tough ones, has a little girl or boy inside of us that needs to be hugged… until the day we die. I have seen plenty of people on their dying hospice bed return to being that little boy. One powerful former banker, as he lay dying at the local hospice facility, looked at his wife in tears and in a small, sheepish voice said, "I want to go home." I never forgot that moment. He's home now.

Living Well

Be oh-so-careful with your words. They tear the very fabric of a person's inner being and torment them as his or her personal tape recorder replays your damaging words for decades.

Try to set up some type of system (I've worked at this for years) where the only thing out of your mouth is uplifting praise. It is so difficult as we fester in a litigious and gossip-laden society. But the peace that will envelope you as you practice this critical skill will be worth the success and lifted spirits that are bound to come.

Everyone will prosper from this: family, friends, and, most of all, your own soul!

"Kind words can be short and easy to speak, but their echoes are truly endless."

Mother Theresa

My Holes-in-the-Fence Checklist
(In whose fence did you leave a hole
that needs repair?)

1. _____

2. _____

3. _____

4. _____

5. _____

Chapter IX

Divine Appointments

I have learned that God schedules *Divine Appointments.*

I was in my final edits of this book when the following incident occurred and I decided to add it here. I was in Chicago (in December 2011) visiting my in-laws. I went to work out at the Oak Forest Park District fitness center and asked an administrator how much it would cost for a single workout. This man, named Bob, remembered me from a few years ago when I spoke to him about the navy reserves. He gave me a free pass as a retired military guy. I could tell Bob had a kind heart so I decided to give him a copy of my book, *Living Well...Making a Difference.*

The next day he enthusiastically let me know what the book meant to him. The day I gifted him he had just had a bad weekend and argued with a relative and did not want to be at work. Then I showed up with the book. He said, "I'm a man of faith and can't help but think that God had a hand in our meeting."

I believe things happen for a reason. I bet you have had moments in your life when you say, "Wow, I can't believe that just happened and am so glad he [or she] was there for me." Or perhaps someone's words or an incident changed your life.

The Bucket List, with two great actors, Morgan Freeman and Jack Nicholson, is one of my favorite movies. If you have not seen it, you need to…because it just may change your life.

Morgan Freeman is a mechanic without much money but he loves his family and friends…*he gets it.* Jack Nicholson is a multi-millionaire who owns several hospitals but whose family is a mess and does not like people…he *doesn't get it.* It is possible to have lots of money and stuff but still get it, but studies show people have more trouble handling success than failure. People often forget their priorities. (I hope you get all that you want but never forget where you came from.)

Both men are dying of cancer and end up together in the same hospital room…by what some people understand as a divine appointment, though the movie does not call it that. Nicholson is upset because he owns the hospital and wonders why he doesn't have a private room. There is a reason. Freeman starts to teach him about life and what really counts. Nicholson decides to fly all over the world to realize his dreams before he "kicks the bucket." He takes Freeman with him because he has begun to like the man.

At the end of the movie, you see Nicholson, after Freeman has died, trying to make amends with those he has hurt or abandoned along the path to success. It's a powerful movie and lesson…a divine appointment.

I cannot begin to tell you how many of these appointments I've had. As a teenager, I volunteered in a local hospital because I wanted to become a doctor. The pharmacist in the hospital told me about ROTC and the naval academy and how I, a poor, young teenager, could get an education. I remember well the day my son Matt decided to attend the naval academy because I took him to a service at their magnificent chapel…another divine appointment. Another time, I had lost my third civilian job and was in desperate financial times when Navy Mutual Aid out of Washington, DC, hired me to give lectures, which started my speaking career. One day a young Southwest Airline pilot ran into me in Nashville and said, "I've heard your message…you've got to write a book." All divine appointments, yet none of these things were on my radar scope at all.

I live my life knowing that divine appointments occur, giving me peace in the knowledge that guidance is coming from something we cannot see. Even though my life does not look like I thought it would, I have peace in knowing that this is the direction my life is supposed to go.

Living Well

It's important to remember that you are part of these divine appointments for others. It's not just about what happens to you! To quote Harold Kushner, "We all hold pieces of the puzzles of other people's lives in our pockets."

Again I refer to my favorite movie, *It's a Wonderful Life,* with Jimmy Stewart. In the movie, George Bailey finds out that not only did he have a wonderful life in his drafty old house, with four kids and a used car and the old Building and Loan, but his life had a profound impact on those around him. The movie is full of divine appointments. Since George was going to commit suicide, Clarence the angel grants him his wish that George Bailey never lived. As a result, George got to see what life would have been without him. The town of Bedford Falls was remarkably different. In one scene, Clarence says, "You see, George, every life touches so many other lives."

Take peace in your divine appointments, both for you and others...it is what makes the masterpiece of life.

"I can't help but think... God had a hand in this."

Bob Bartkowski,
Oak Forest Fitness Center

My "*Divine Appointments*" Checklist

(What *Divine Appointments* have happened in your life?)

1. _____

2. _____

3. _____

4. _____

5. _____

Chapter X

Physical Fitness

I have learned that physical fitness has vastly improved my quality of life.

In *Living Well...Making a Difference,* I did not mention physical fitness because that book was focused on impacting others, not yourself. You now know your life greatly improves when you help others.

As I grow older, I have found I have better health and more stamina to serve others than many of my contemporaries. I attribute that to having taken care of my body as well as I could have, even though I am decaying much faster now than in my younger days.

It has not always been easy to drag myself out of bed early in the morning, or pass up lunch with the guys, or take a jog on a blistering summer afternoon.

But this is one habit that I'm glad I have. Okay, so I do have several bad ones, too. ("Hi, my name's Andy... and I'm a chocoholic.")

Cindy says I have a compulsion complex. Or as Barney Fife said on one episode of the *Andy Griffith Show*, "The guy has a compelsion complex, you know, like a hand 'warshing' compelsion." If I miss a couple of days of working out, I start to get cranky and Cindy knows I need a workout. I encourage you to adopt some program to raise your heart rate. You might find that you, too, will get addicted to the wonderful feeling of getting that blood flowing and the endorphins generated.

I see people every day who are literally eating themselves to death. They are eating into immobility and severely degrading their quality of life. Sometimes the American lifestyle isn't so good for us. When you super-size your meal, you are supersizing your waistline. I do not mean to be placing a guilt complex on anyone and I am not trying to make you feel terrible if you don't look like one of those models in those fitness ads. I can't believe some of those companies are not sued for false advertising. That guy with the picture-perfect "six-pack" stomach did NOT get that way on that machine they are trying to get you to buy. He has spent hours each day in a gym pumping iron hard and has disciplined his diet. Have you ever seen how many hours it takes to run off a Snickers bar? The most important step to take is pushing yourself away from the table.

Besides the health benefits, you will feel so much better mentally. You will be more confident when your clothes fit better. Your mind will feel terrific at the end of a workout—not just self-confidence but also clearing out some of those cobwebs. There are tons of studies to back this concept up.

As a public speaker, I find that an important aspect of a presentation is the non-verbal aspect: my expressions, body language, and personal appearance. When I feel better physically, I have more energy to make that one-time impact.

I had a physical at the navy hospital a few years back and asked one of my favorite doctors of all time, Rowena Papson, "Doc, my joints are starting to bother me. Should I stop running?" She said, "No, it will get worse from inactivity, plus the mental impact will lead to possible depression." I gave her a huge hug because I did not want to quit running. I was still playing ice hockey last year at age fifty-six...granted, the young'uns skated circles around me but I loved the exercise and competitive atmosphere. It was kind of neat to be a warrior just one more time.

Here are a few tips and thoughts for you. As I mentioned, pushing away from the table does more for your waistline than a workout, but you need both; they complement each other. Don't supersize! I never had to worry about gaining weight when I was younger but now the battle of the bulge is a reality with me. I turn down those fries now and go with single sandwiches on whole wheat...it's still good! To feed my chocolate fetish, I go with dark chocolate, which is less fattening and has anti-oxidants (my excuse). I do enjoy a cold beer and now go with the lowest-carb choice. I am not living a monk's life by any means but you have to think moderation, especially when that metabolism slows down. Your grandkids and great-grandkids will love you for it. Got to think smaller portions and drinking more water. Water suppresses the appetite and helps flush out the system.

Now for raising that heart rate, start by taking a beautiful walk in the morning…it may evolve to a slow jog. Playing tennis, bowling, bike riding, swimming—there are all kinds of things that are low-impact for your joints plus many end up being social events with PEOPLE that add to your joy. Win-win! In addition, you enjoy the beautiful outdoors in many cases.

We also have to get the kids away from too much of the video games. We cannot dismiss the importance of physical fitness in their lives at an early age. Childhood obesity is a problem. When I was a kid, we played army, baseball, football, etc…until Mom came after us with the belt if we were late for dinner. Now the only exercise most kids get is in their fingers. That's okay in MODERATION, but I think it is way out of whack. Moreover, they need the social interaction away from cyberspace to make them successful and well-adjusted adults.

I hope I have provided some incentive and wanted to let you in on a very important aspect of my happiness. You do not need to look like a body builder or magazine model. Those men and women have their issues, too. I just want to remind you of the tremendous benefits of some type of physical activity. Your friends and family will notice and all aspects of a life lived well will multiply.

Body, mind, spirit! Go get 'em!

Physical Fitness

"Those who think they have no time for bodily exercise will sooner or later have to find time for illness."

Edward Stanley
(1826-1893)
British Prime Minister

Living Well

My Physical Fitness Checklist
(List some things you're going to
start doing to break a sweat!)

1. _____

2. _____

3. _____

4. _____

5. _____

64

Chapter XI

Little Things Mean A Lot

I've learned that the small gestures of kindness in life, the things we often pay no attention to, really mean a lot.

Most people go through life unengaged, just trudging along day after day, heading for their final appointment with a hospice bed. I call them "the walking dead"...just existing. Opportunities for random acts of kindness pass them by constantly. If they would take advantage of these opportunities, they would find that small acts of kindness warm their spirit and also make them feel better inside.

In my seminar, I talk about a depressed man whose psychiatrist's prescription was to compliment three people each day. He said, "What, me compliment

others? I'm the one who needs the compliments!"
However, it had a remarkable impact on the man's
attitude and demeanor as he executed the prescription. Your spirit is fed by helping others. That's just the
way it works. A couple months ago at one of my talks,
a clinical psychologist from Georgia was in the crowd
and confirmed my point. She said she often tells her
patients the same thing. People have got to "*get it*" that
life is not about them.

Just think about the difference in how you feel
when someone cuts you off in traffic and makes a bad
hand gesture as opposed to someone who lets you
merge into traffic. Even better, how about when you
let them merge and see them pop one of my thank-you
paddles out of their window? It warms your heart and
your spirit smiles.

Think about how you feel when someone smiles
at you in the local grocery store and asks how you are
today as opposed to many who scowl at you and won't
even give you the time of day.

As I write this chapter, I am on vacation at one
of our favorite places on earth called Summerhouse
Condos in Crescent Beach, Florida. The woman in
the condo next to us is named Leigh. I gave her a
copy of *Living Well...Making a Difference,* as I often do
when someone touches my heart with kindness. After
reading it, she had to tell me of an incident in Tulsa,
Oklahoma. As she was sitting at a traffic light in a foul
mood with a scowl on her face, she noticed a young
man across from her at the light in an old beat-up car.
He mockingly returned her scowl but then took his

fingers and manually turned his frown into a warm smile…hoping it would provoke a smile on her face, which it did. This young man, who was obviously not very well-off, had made a small gesture that changed her day and, frankly, she said often her outlook on life. Little things mean a lot.

Or how about the single mom standing with her two cranky kids fifteen deep in the post office line at Christmas and the guy at the front of the line trades places with her? This is a small gesture for the retired guy with all day to give, but a big deal to the single mom who is absolutely swamped and about to lose it.

Think about how you feel if you get a birthday card, but instead of the usual, "Have a happy birthday…love so and so," it has a few words about how you have influenced their life. It's a small gesture with a big impact. I know we all send tons of cards out with no gift because only a few family members are on our gift list for birthdays. However, I have started a new tactic and thrown in a fast-food gift certificate. I am amazed at how people have thanked me and enjoyed this inexpensive gesture. The next time they go to my favorite Scottish restaurant—McDonald's—or BK, Wendy's, or wherever, they remember it was on me and they smile at that small act of kindness…pretty cool!

My wife, Cindy, is good at this…I learn from her all the time. She loves to cook meals for the sick or sew things for people or take on tasks they are unable to do on the computer or wherever. The neatest thing about her gestures is she often does not want them to know who did it…or has me run the food over. Have to love the humility.

When I was commanding officer of my last squadron, I would write little notes on my personal stationery to any sailor who did something above and beyond the normal call of duty. I told my staff to keep an eye out for these acts and report them to me if they noticed any. Another leadership principle I subscribed to was LBWA (leadership by walking around). I wanted to let people know that I knew they existed and what they did was important. Too many commanding officers and CEOs stay cooped up in their big office, not giving the deck plate worker the time of day…big mistake. I think this *Undercover Boss* on TV is such a great concept. It gives the boss the opportunity to see what really goes on. I used to learn more about what was really happening in the squadron at happy hour at the chiefs' or officers' club than at the squadron spaces. But back to my point: I would often see my little notes FRAMED on their desks in the squadron spaces. Little things mean a lot.

I would also randomly show up in the middle of the night (2:00 AM) to see how the night shift people were doing. Lost a little sleep but gained a lot in respect and motivation of the troops. I acknowledged them as human beings and let them know what they did was important to their country and me. Little things mean a lot.

Note cards and especially the words inside are powerful. When I visited Mayberry Days in Mount Airy North Carolina (Andy Griffith's hometown), I found the neatest little note cards with a stippling (dot matrix) of Andy, Opie, and Barney fishing at Meyers Lake. They are all looking over their shoulders and you can just feel the peace in the picture. Just looking at the picture makes life's stresses leave my body. The artist is a woman named Loretta Stewart, who lives on Bobcat Hollow Road, Parkersburg, West Virginia...how appropriate. They have become my trademark whenever I want to thank someone for dinner or an act of kindness or just let them know I am thinking of them.

I sent one of these cards to a friend named Dennis a few months ago who has cancer now. They have already removed one lung and the chemo treatment is in progress. He works at the Naval Air Station Jax Commissary, one of my favorite places on earth because it is full of wonderful people. Dennis is a kind and peaceful man who is pushing sixty years of age. I just wanted to let him know what his friendship has meant to me, how he has made a difference, and how he will continue to impact lives in the future. He saw me a few weeks after the note, hugged me with tears in his eyes, and let me know what my note meant to him. He said, "You don't know how much notes like that mean when you are on the *other side* of cancer." (January 2012 update: Dennis is in Heaven.)

I rest my case...little things mean a lot.

"To the loved, a word of affection is a morsel, but to the loved-starved, a word of affection can be a feast."

Max Lucado

My "Little Things Mean a Lot" Checklist
(List the little things you can do to impact people's joy.)

1. _____

2. _____

3. _____

4. _____

5. _____

Chapter XII

We're All A "Sight"

I have learned that we are all a mess.

We all have issues, hang-ups, and things we wouldn't want anyone to know about. I think every family is dysfunctional in its own way. John Ortberg describes this phenomenon best in his book titled *Everyone's Normal Till You Get to Know Them*.

In one of the old black-and-white *Andy Griffith* episodes (my favorites), Opie comes into the courthouse after rough-housing with some kids on the playground. His clothes are tattered and his face is full of mud. Andy asks what he's been doing and Opie says he was wrestling with some of his buddies. Andy says, "You're a sight."

Living Well

I have a wonderful friend named Vic Halbach in my men's small group, and one night I used this term and he said, "I have not heard that term since I was a kid in the hills of eastern Tennessee." (That's close to Mount Airy...Mayberry, by the way.)

My pastor uses a different term for the same concept; he mentions in many sermons that we are all a mess, we are all broken in some way or another.

I definitely think most of our spiritual and mental makeup is good but we all struggle with this fleshly body and wanting to do bad things for our body and spirit.

Too many of us overeat, get too much sun, lose our temper, have addictions, have too many beers, gossip, watch something we shouldn't, overspend, hold grudges, covet, get materialistic...I could go on and on.

Please remember we're all a sight. And before the eyes of God you are no better or worse than the next fellow. Their overeating is no worse than your lust or jealousy of your neighbors. Sometimes their problem is just more visible, isn't it?

When I first heard my pastor talk about this and got to know men through different church and social groups and read John Ortberg's book, it was very freeing for me to know that I'm not the only one who is a mess. I guess "mess" is also a relative term. Some people have more issues than others. A friend of mine is a psychologist. He once told me how damaging a physically and/or emotionally abusive childhood can be for the remainder of a person's life. Who knows what some folks have been through? So it's important to make sure you love and discipline your kids. Also, try to keep your "discussions" with your spouse out of their earshot. Your marriage has a direct impact on the foundation of their emotional lives.

Don't we all also tend to be critical of others at times, judgmental, holier than thou, or whatever you want to call it? Well, the guy I tend to be hardest on is myself. I suspect I am now speaking to many of you who are the same way. I have laid awake too many nights tormenting myself over past mistakes and failures. I am a man laden with sin and failures. However, it has been so relieving to know that I am not alone and my faith gives me hope.

Some of the most powerful and influential men in the Bible were also a mess. Moses killed a man in Egypt yet led the Jewish people out of slavery. David had a child out of wedlock and had his mistress's husband killed; he was perhaps Israel's greatest king and was in the lineage of Jesus. Paul was a persecutor and killer of Christians and when he finally *got it,* ended up writing most of the New Testament. These stories should give us all hope.

Whenever I catch myself judging someone, my little voice quickly reminds me of my millions of sins and I think, *Who am I to judge?* Jesus often went after the Pharisees in the Bible, who supposedly were the holiest members of Jewish society yet were often the most hypocritical with their judgments and how they treated people. There may be some folks reading this thinking, *Well, Andy, I don't have any addictions, or "compelsions" or phobias…I don't swear, go to the dark side of the Internet, lose my temper, overeat…I pretty much have it all together.* I hope you do, but it's just possible you might be seeing pride creep in, thinking you are better than others perhaps. Be careful, be humble, and just treat people like you would like to be treated.

No matter what you have done, what childhood scars you have to deal with, addictions you cannot break, temper you are trying to control, there is a path of continuous improvement you can't give up on. You were born with a spirit that knows right from wrong and how good it feels when you are on track. Keep striving. It's worth the fight. When you fail, get up and keep trying. I was amazed at how many times Abraham Lincoln failed to get elected in his political career. He did not give up and thank God he didn't. He was perhaps our greatest president at a time the nation desperately needed him.

Billy Graham's wife, Ruth Graham Bell, died a few years ago. Before she died, she saw a sign at the end of a construction zone in North Carolina that said, "End of construction, thank you for your patience." She put those words on her tombstone. End of construction, thank you for your patience. We are all under construction until the day we die, and God knows I hope people are patient with me.

The day you depart this earth, the hospice nurse coming to change your sheets may be contemplating taking her life that night. The words you say to her near the end may push her one way or the other. You are important and will have an impact to the very end.

I have done many good things and many bad things in my life. I know that I have been blessed more than I deserve. I love how financial guru Dave Ramsey puts it: "I am doing better than I deserve." And because of that feeling, I have this unquenchable drive to improve this earth and everyone I run into before my transition to a better place. I need you to help and please don't let your mess get in the way.

Let's go easy on each other and ourselves and keep the construction going. You are a miracle and there will never be another you. The world needs us to be the best we can be. After all, we are but a wisp in time.

"Devote yourself to this one task, to loving 'as-is people,' and no matter what else you may not achieve, you will lead a magnificent life."

John Ortberg

We're All a Sight Checklist
(List the things you need to
forgive yourself for and move forward.)

1. _____

2. _____

3. _____

4. _____

5. _____

Chapter XIII

Never Say "Never"

I have learned to never say "never"…things that I thought could not possibly come true have come to fruition.

On the south side of Chicago in a fairly rough side of town during the 1960s, golf was not a big sport. Nobody in my neighborhood played the game. Kids played lots of football, baseball, and hockey, but not much golf. However, one day an older neighbor, a teenager named Butch Sopher, took me and his little brother, John, to a golf course to watch him play. It was a little nine-hole course called Dandelion Hill, I think. It was soon replaced in the late '60s by Dixie Square Mall in Harvey, Illinois. I think this ended up being the mall destroyed by the Blues Brothers in the movie before it was torn down.

Anyhow, I was so impressed by the smoothness of the grass on the green that I decided to pursue the game. I remember that day so clearly: getting on my hands and knees to feel the grass and how beautifully kept that little patch of grass was. So, for my birthday, I asked for a putter, three balls, and two of those silver metal peddled golf holes that the ball trickles into and corrals it in the center. I put them at the ends of my hallway in that small home in Markham, Illinois. I had the balls compete against each other and named them Arnold Palmer, Jack Nicklaus, and Ken Venturi, three hot golf names in the 1960s. I thought to myself, *I'll never meet one of them.* Never say "never."

I ended up making the high school varsity golf team as a freshman. The tryouts were the first time I had ever played on a real golf course. I taught myself the game in a field behind McClaughry School just down the street from my house. Don't be too impressed…golf was small potatoes at Bremen High School and I still sport a seventeen handicap.

As my life unfolded, I pursued a career as a naval aviator. In 1986, I had a job as a catapult officer on the *USS John F. Kennedy* aircraft carrier. One day the captain of the ship, Jack Moriarity, who knew I was kind of a golfer, asked me for a favor. (By the way, when the captain of the ship asks you for a favor, you have no choice☺.) He asked me to escort a friend of his, Ken Venturi, 1964 US Open winner and *CBS Sports* announcer, for a week and be his personal aide. Never say "never."

Never Say "Never"

Mr. Venturi and I hit it off and have been friends ever since. He spoke at the change-of-command ceremony of my first squadron and at my retirement from the navy in the World Golf Hall of Fame, where he will be inducted in May of 2013. He is a wonderfully kind gentleman who has shown me how humble and giving a celebrity can be.

Never say "never." One of my favorite stories to reinforce this concept occurred at my alma mater, the United States Naval Academy, in 1996. We were attending a church service at the magnificent chapel at Annapolis and it was a moving service for me. I saw people I had not seen in twenty years and I had wet eyes through most of the service. My high school senior son, Matt, could see I was moved. As we left the church service, I still remember where we were standing; he said, "Dad, what can you do to help me get in this place?"

I was very shocked. It was late in his senior year and he was not taking math or science (heavy academy requirements). He lacked some of the required extra-curricular activities, never liked following rules, getting up early in the morning, or studying. In my eyes, not a good fit for the naval academy, so I discouraged it. I would love to have a son follow my footsteps but did not think this was right for Matt.

But Matt was determined and because I was familiar with the process, I had him in front of the right people the next week for admission. They said he had very little hope, as I suspected...but Matt interviewed well and is a smart kid who tests well. He qualified for a presidential appointment because of my alumni and active duty status, but he did not get a direct appointment that year. However, he did well enough to win a scholarship to a prep school, where all he had to do was pass and he was in the next year (a red shirt freshman, so to speak). However, I had to pick up twelve thousand dollars of the prep school tuition, which was a year's worth of the college money I had saved and a year of his life. Plus, if he quit plebe year, which I thought was a good possibility, I would have to pick up the other twenty-two thousand dollars, which would bring the total to three years' worth of college money (back then). Wow, talk about high risk, high gain.

But despite my fears, he made it through the academy and did well in the military flying the same aircraft I did. He actually did more than I ever did…risking his life flying multiple combat missions in Afghanistan. Never say "never."

After completing his service requirement, Matt decided to leave the navy in the middle of the worst economic crisis in America since the depression; it is being called the Great Recession. This was despite my recommendations to him to stay in the service, as his naval career was tracking well and I feared he may never get a decent civilian job at that time. Plus, he had a family to feed. He ended up landing a super job with Chesapeake Energy Corporation and is doing very well. Never say "never."

Never Say "Never"

When the navy placed me in Florida for most of my career, I quickly saw that college football was bigger than the NFL here. Since the naval academy was far away and struggles to compete with D1 football programs, I knew I needed to pick a college team to align with, as everyone had one. Bill Marriott, a good friend who was the third pilot on our crew, was a fanatic about the Florida Gators, so I went with them. My kids and I both grew to like the Gators and had the shirts and jerseys. We all hated Florida State. Well, my youngest son, Brad, ended up going to Florida State for various reasons...so the team I said I would NEVER like was where my money started heading. Instead of the Gator chomp I had to learn the tomahawk chop! God knew what Brad needed. He met his lovely bride, Christy Keith, at Florida State and she has been a huge blessing to him and all the family...plus they just gave us a handsome grandson named Evan, Celtic for "the little warrior." Never say "never."

Don't worry, Brad, my sports fanatical son, FSU's football program will be back, probably before the Chicago Cubs. But you gained what is the most important aspect of life besides your faith, and that is the partner with whom you share your life. Never say "never."

"If had I only knew, I could have missed the pain, but then I would have had to miss the dance."

Garth Brooks

My Never Say "Never" Checklist
(Times you should have never said "never.")

1. _____

2. _____

3. _____

4. _____

5. _____

Chapter XIV

Contentment

I have learned that contentment is really what most people strive for in life...some of them just don't know it.

I once heard Chuck Swindoll give a sermon and he talked about happiness, joy, and contentment. He contends that we all seek a deep-seated feeling of contentment. Occasionally you see people who have an air of peace around them that exudes from their soul and you gravitate toward them. They seem to have found that contentment.

Happiness actually comes from the word "*happens.*" Most people's moods and inner joy seem to be driven by what is going on in their life—in other words, by what is happening. Good things spawn a happy day but a bad day at the office or with the kids spawns the downtrodden look, cutting people off in traffic, and a scowl at an intersection or neighborhood grocery store.

In moving toward contentment, I have noticed many people seem to have moved beyond happiness and possess joy. I think of joy as an inner feeling of being happy with who you are, what you do, loving family and friends for who they are and where they're at in life (kind of how our dog loves us… unconditional love). Joyful people see the beauty in small, simple things and realize they don't need more square footage to live in or a more expensive hunk of metal to move them from point A to point B. They treat people the way they want to be treated. This is not a hard concept; rather, this is how life works. When you *get it* and understand this concept, it brings contentment. It brings relief from stress and a feeling of peace. Contentment brings the recognition that this is my life unfolding now, no matter what I thought it should be… *this is my life as God intended.*

In the New Testament, Paul, who was killing Christians, becomes a devoted follower of Christ and in one of his letters wrote, "I know what it is to be in need and I know what it is to have plenty. I have learned the secret of being content in any and every situation, whether well fed or hungry, whether living in plenty or in want" (1). In other words, he understood that his faith, applying Christ's teachings, and helping others was what really mattered. In order to be content, he did not need the things we all get caught up in, and neither do we.

Contentment

Today as I look out on this beautiful ocean at Crescent Beach, I realize I am now finally moving to a state of contentment. This has happened because my faith has grown and taught me that there is a much better place after leaving this earth. I have learned, finally, many of the concepts I wanted to discuss in this book. I am learning to forgive myself because we are all a mess. I am finally slowing it down. It is a relief to be who I am. I wish I could jump like Michael Jordan or hit a drive like Phil Mickelson, but I can't. Instead of trying to fix things around the house, now I call the handyman because I know I can't fix things: a macho thing with many men. I'm over it. My computer skills are lacking as I struggle just to use Microsoft Word to put my thoughts on paper, so I know working for Intel or Microsoft is not in my future. I am not a detail guy and had to hire my detail-oriented wife to keep my books. This is my life...a non-detailed, acne scarred, average slug, retired sailor who loves to dabble in writing and occasionally speaking to help people along life's path. No corporate corner office...but a great wife and two wonderful sons, daughter-in-laws, and grandbabies. I have enough *stuff,* but, more important, I have people who love me (thank God...'cuz I'm a sight) and have met men and women along life's path who get it and have made *my life rich...with their hearts.*

This contentment is well within your reach. Understanding many of these concepts and accepting who you are will go a long way toward helping you achieve that goal. Realizing that this is your life and these are the people in your sphere of influence will help the peace creep into your soul.

Living Well

I am living the dash that will be etched between my birth and death dates on my tombstone. I do not get another life. This is it, folks...how are you living your dash? Live in the precious present and enjoy each breath God gives you.

> *"Life is what happens while you are planning your future."*

> *Anon*

My Contentment Checklist
(Things you will do or accept to move toward contentment)

1. _____

2. _____

3. _____

4. _____

5. _____

Chapter XV

The Old Man's Check-Up

I have learned not to save my nice blue shirts.

In my first book, I wrote about my great neighbor Garo, whom I nicknamed "Wilson" after *Home Improvement*'s Tim Taylor's backyard fence neighbor. As you may know, the Wilson on TV was kind, philosophical, and always had time for Tim. Garo was like that to me.

Well, tragically, my Wilson died on April 16, 2011. He had hospice care near the end and I was trying to spend as much time with him as he was able to stay awake. He said something to me near the end that had a profound impact on my philosophy on life. It was such a simple statement that quite possibly had much more behind it than he realized.

Living Well

Wilson was wearing a nice dry-fit blue shirt (my favorite color) and I complimented him on it. He said, "Yeah, it's one of my best shirts that I was saving...but I don't know what I was saving it for." He died about four days after that statement.

I have a friend, Dr. Sue Hennigan, who loves champagne and she once said, "I don't save it for special occasions anymore. I have it when I want it and I drink it from my best crystal." Do you know where I am going with this? Stay with me.

Throughout this book, I have discussed how material things do not buy happiness and how much joy comes into your life when you focus on the important things. Maybe some of my readers or audience participants think I'm suggesting they live in a double-wide and drive a fifteen-year-old Saturn to enjoy their life. But please remember it is perfectly okay to have stuff. The problem is many of us become obsessed and let our possessions own us. I believe there is a happy balance. You should have and enjoy a reasonable measure of *stuff* throughout your life and not save it all for the end.

This reminds me of the old man who goes to the hospital for a check-up and a blood test. The doctor comes in to give the old man his test results. He states that the old man's blood sugar is low, cholesterol is down, red blood cell count is good, etc. He tells him he should easily live to be eighty-five. The old man says, "Well, that is terrific and makes sense because I have never had a steak, I don't put butter on my popcorn, never had any chocolate or ice cream, I don't drink beer, and never touch French fries." The doctor looks at him in amazement and says, "Why would you want to live 'til you're eighty-five?"

There are two ways to live that are at opposite ends of the spectrum. One is overindulgence and one is deprivation. I have known people who save every penny and live with just the bare minimums but plan on building their dream house at age sixty-five or are set on being called a millionaire someday. The problem is many of the people they want to impress will already be dead. I have also known people who always have new cars every few years, the biggest house, nicest clothes, eat out all the time but have very little in the bank. That brings self-perpetuated stress. There is a happy medium. Enjoy the times after you are newly married, when your kids are home, when they are in college, when you have your health, being grandparents...in other words, enjoy your entire life—all the seasons of life.

Over 1.2 million brave Americans have given their lives so that we may enjoy ours and make a difference to others. They did not die for you to be a brooding, mean-spirited, arrogant, self-centered person. There is so much joy to be had in every breath...it is your mindset and your choice.

At the end of the movie *Saving Private Ryan*, Tom Hanks, who portrays an army captain, has found Private Ryan, the last brother of four, so the parents have at least one boy remaining. As Hanks lies mortally wounded on a bridge in France, he pulls Private Ryan (Matt Damon) to his side and in his last dying breath says, "Earn it." Fast forward to Ryan as an old man walking the cemetery on Normandy beach and he finds the grave of the army captain that saved his life. He says, "I hope I earned it and I will never forget what you did for me." He turns to his wife and says, "Tell me I was a good man and lived a good life."

I love dark chocolate, a cold beer, butter on my popcorn, Burger King Whoppers with cheese, IN-N-OUT "animal fries," and on and on, but I also make sure I get my vitamins in the morning, eat some fruit, have veggies (sometimes), and also try to break a sweat every day doing something. I am far from perfect and occasionally go too far one way or the other but I do try to maintain a balance that adds to my quality of life. When you do that, your healthy body and soul bless others.

Time goes fast, my friend. It's kind of like a roll of toilet paper: the closer you get to the end, the faster it goes.

As I have heard so many waiters or waitresses say when they bring my meal, "Enjoy!"

"I went into the woods because I wished to live deliberately…and not, when I came to die, discover that I had not lived."

Henry David Thoreau

The Old Man's Check-Up

My "Old Man's Check-up" Checklist
(Noticed I doubled this one.)
(Things you will do to enjoy your life)

1. _____

2. _____

3. _____

4. _____

5. _____

6. _____

7. _____

8. _____

9. _____

10. _____

Chapter XVI

Be Who You Are

I have learned to be Andy Andersen and not someone else. To take down the veneer or façade and be who God intended me to be. It is one of the most freeing lessons I have learned in my life.

As I wrote the title of this chapter, it just occurred to me that this is another Kenny Chesney song, "Be Who You Are." It's about not putting up a front but just being that unique individual God intended you to be. Nobody else has your exact set of genes…or ever will.

This is such a critical area to our own peace of mind and joy. Most people seem to put up façades of who their boss, or social group, or country club, or society says they're supposed to be or act like or talk like or dress like or drive... *to be somebody.*

Puts a lot of stress and strain on the mind, body, and spirit to try to conform to something you're not. I have struggled with this big-time since I left the military over eleven years ago. It has caused deep anguish and pain that I need to share with you. It's been a huge life lesson for me.

In 2003, after I lost my third job, I was feeling depressed, wondering where I fit in this crazy world. Through these struggles, I decided to see my pastor, Kevin Pound, to see if he could help me figure out what in the heck was going on with my life. Why don't I seem to fit?

As I sat across from him, I distinctly remember one question he asked me that has had a profound effect on my peace of mind and newfound joy. He looked at me and asked, "Who are you?"

Well, "I'm Andy Andersen, Pastor. You know that." He asked again, "No, who are you really?" In other words, 'What's in your heart, where is your passion, what do you enjoy, where are your skill sets, and what gives you joy in being the unique Andy Andersen?'

You see, I felt I had to portray a certain image, maybe be driving my Lexus or Cadillac by then and climbing the corporate ladder. So I would hide the fact that I hate being cooped up in a cubicle with a desktop computer and that my biorhythms do not get along with electrons. I stink at computer stuff and technology. I need to be out somewhere making a difference somehow in people's lives…whether it's volunteer work or a minimum-wage job at Publix bagging groceries. I need to be *with people* and adjust my lifestyle to fit where my passion lies.

I am now comfortable being me. I tried to be like so many of my contemporaries who have landed and succeeded at powerful jobs and have more stuff than I'll see in my lifetime. As it turns out, that was not in the cards. I continue to be a buy-high/sell-low kind of guy. It's time to stop wasting heartbeats on trying to fit society's mold of what I thought I should be. It is time to accept "my gap."

I can't tell you how fulfilled I am when I share life stories with a room full of people. I can feel a force of satisfaction flow through me in knowing I am doing what I was meant to do in my short time on this earth. In John Ortberg's book *The Me I Want to Be*, he describes this condition as "flow" because people experiencing it often feel like they are being swept up in something greater than themselves (1).

Ortberg also mentions that Marcus Aurelios of ancient Rome wrote, "When you arise reluctantly in the morning, think like this, 'I arise to accomplish a human task. Should I then complain, when I am about to do that for which I was born, and for which I was placed on this earth? Or was I created to pamper myself under the blankets, even if that is more pleasant.' Were you born, then, to enjoy and, generally to feel, but not act? Don't you see the plants, the birds, the ants, the spiders, the bees who all perform their own tasks and in their own way helping to let the cosmos function? Don't you then want to do your work as a human? Don't you hasten to do what is befitting your nature?" (2)

Absolutely love that quote: beautiful summation of doing what you were meant to do…doing your part.

It's very freeing to admit that I am not good at most things. Give me a basketball I'm like a three-legged elephant on ice. But give me a set of horseshoes and I'll whip most folks. I feel pretty good with a four iron in my hand or a hockey stick…but give me a set of detailed instructions to follow and I break out in hives. You really enjoy life when you do what you were meant to do. You can tell when you are in the groove or, as John Ortberg says, in the flow. I have seen good friends who are superb pilots, have a passion for it, and still do it. God bless 'em. It was not my passion. I miss the people aspect of the military. I am so thankful for the head hunter who gave me that personality/skill set test and told me I was not fit for certain jobs. I just thought I was to fit a typical post-navy career. Nope. I was fit to be Andy Andersen…this unique set of chromosomes that no one else will ever be. Those who know me pray for my wife for having to live with me daily. Thank God Cindy and I lived within our means and have the latitude to now pursue our passions.

In the New Testament, the disciple Paul said, "Do not be conformed to the pattern of this world, but be transformed by the renewing of your mind" (3). For a person to experience lasting peace and joy, they must change how they think. Focus on what really counts. That was my New Year's resolution for 2011: renew my mind. I have got to rid my mind of the thoughts that dominate many men—bigger houses, faster cars, younger women, more power…all the things that steal your joy. Just be me and accomplish my task. Your thoughts become actions that become character and then become who you are…and those will be the footprints that remain.

It might surprise some of you that the author of a book and motivation presentation titled *Living Well…Making a Difference* has these thoughts. Well, it's because I am also a man filled with sin, pride, ego, and fighting all the battles that all men fight. However, I also know these principles work. I am so glad I am not the man I used to be but also know I have a long way to go. I am under construction until the day I die.

You were put on this earth in your situation to fulfill your destiny and make an impact. Those who only care about themselves will never fulfill their destiny, realize their full potential, or understand why they were put here. God did not put you here for you. You were put here to impact other lives, as Jackie Robinson so beautifully inscribed on his tombstone: "A life is not important except for the impact it has on other lives." To help people through this crazy thing called life…to impact the people in *your* sphere of influence.

Again I refer to Ken Graham, the grocery bagger in my first book; that man, with his simple job of carrying people's groceries to their cars, filled countless people's lives with joy…and you can do that, too.

Living Well

Be who you are, pursue your passion, renew your mind. The world needs _you_!

"Be who you are and say what you feel, because those who mind don't matter and those who matter don't mind."

Dr. Seuss

Be Who You Are

My "Be Who You Are" Checklist
(What parts of your façade need to come down?)

1. _____

2. _____

3. _____

4. _____

5. _____

Chapter XVII

The Old Rifle Stock

I've learned that one man's junk can be another man's treasure. Want what you have.

When I was a child around eight to ten years old, the neighborhood boys and I loved to play army. The Petersons, John Sopher, the Butlers, the Karas, and I would play all day down at the end of the street in a field we called "The Jackpot." I guess we called it that because we were always finding food or some abandoned possessions of perhaps a homeless person. So, we kids thought we hit the jackpot when we found a few stray coins or food.

Anyhow, this wooded, half-block area was perfect for playing army. (And I ended up being a navy guy!) We would divide into good and bad guys and search each other out. It was a lot of fun and exercise and something that so many kids are missing now. We would usually get new toy guns for Christmas and they would last us a year or so…not long enough, according to our parents.

About that time, my dad and Uncle Ray used to hunt pheasants, ducks, and deer quite a bit. I always remember my dad talking about his "thirty-oh-six." I think that meant "3006"…forgive me, gun guys. But that was a high-powered rifle they used.

One day my uncle Ray (he just passed into Heaven in June 2011) came over to the house and gave me an old shell of a rifle. It was just the wooden stock, if you can picture that, without the gun barrel. I was very excited— like a real gun! (Seems back then we enjoyed small things much more, as we have slowly gotten used to *more stuff* as a society.) So that became my new army gun.

As I played with the old rifle stock, I became dis-enchanted with it, having no barrel in it, and started to let the other kids know it was up for grabs. My next-door neighbor, Jack Butler, said he would take it, and off the old rifle stock went.

Well, my buddy Jack decided to use some good old ingenuity and cut off an old broom stick. He placed the broom stick in the stock like a barrel and taped it in with a bunch of masking tape. I can still picture that gun forty-five years later. It looked sharp and, boy, did I *regret my decision to let her go.*

So, like a typical kid, I wanted back what really wasn't mine anymore. I pouted and let Jack know I would like it back. I remember him saying, "Of course, now that I fixed it up, Bobby [my real first name is Robert] wants it back." I felt like an Indian giver, but I wanted her back bad.

How many times have you seen a small child want what another kid has even though their own toy box is overflowing? I'm not sure that we ever get over that ingrained "got to have" or at least "keep up with the Joneses" mentality. Not happy with what we have and unable to count our blessings.

I just love that old rifle stock metaphor. How many marriages have been destroyed over wanting the faster, younger model or something someone else has? I'm thinking after a few years, the new spouse rolls over in bed and says, "Did you take the trash out?" and you're right back where you were before because we get used to everything. I have also noticed that a lot of divorcees lose weight through their trials and end up looking really good. But, unfortunately, now the train has left the station, and the old rifle stock is looking awfully good but pouting probably won't bring them back.

This concept played itself out again in my life recently. Carrying books and thank-you paddles to my speaking engagements, I have limited space in my old Mustang convertible. I started to look for another car, a small SUV to carry my wares. I decided on a Hyundai Tucson for its affordability, reliability, and looks. Had it all and supports my concept of not spending too much on a depreciating asset.

I fell in love with a black one in St. Augustine, Florida. I got a great price, wrote the check, and said I would pick it up the next day. But that night, I had no peace. I could not sleep and kept getting up to look at my old "friend" in the garage who had taken me through many tough times in my life, both financial and employment issues, and could not get rid of her.

I called my bank the next day, stopped the check, called the shocked dealer, and said I didn't want the car. I have yet to speak to a group where I can't pack enough stuff in my Mustang, the old Red Rocket, to offer the audience. I was talking myself into it, plus I did not like the idea of new car payments or depleting my savings…I hate debt.

So the old rifle stock Red Rocket is still serving me well; she has well over two hundred and forty thousand miles on her. I have yet to change the starter, water pump, or alternator.

I had an old man sitting in a car next to me at a stop light the other day. I had my top down and he seemed to be admiring my car. He said, "Beautiful little Mustang." I said, "She's sixteen years old with two hundred thousand miles." He said, "That's okay. I'd like to put another hundred thousand on her."

Not sure how much longer she'll last, but for now I think I'll put the broom stick in the old rifle stock and just keep my old, reliable friend.

"Happiness comes from being content with what you have."

Anon

My Rifle Stock Checklist
(Old things that are serving you well and
are worth keeping)

1. _____

2. _____

3. _____

4. _____

5. _____

Chapter XVIII

The Andersen Dairy

**Charles, Bill, and Lowell Andersen,
Omaha, Nebraska, circa 1900**

I've learned that when you skim the cream off the top of life for yourself, you really deprive yourself and others of blessings.

According to family history, my great-grandfather, Peter Andersen, came to the United States around

1868 from Copenhagen, Denmark. He took a train from New York to Iowa and settled in the Omaha, Nebraska, area. He was a baker by trade and worked in an Omaha bakery.

He married an American Indian named Mary Buttrick; to the best of my knowledge she came from a Chippewa tribe near Leech Lake in Minnesota. They had three kids: Charlie, Lawrence, and Bill Andersen. They ended up divorcing supposedly due to my great-grandfather's difficult personality and the three small children ended up in a home for boys. At one point my grandfather, Bill Andersen, was about six years old and is said to have had beautiful, blond, curly hair. This would have been around 1900 or the turn of the twentieth century. Well, one day a family decided to adopt this cute little boy. But his brother, my great-uncle, Charlie, who was about ten years old at the time, was not going to let them be separated. So he took my grandfather, Bill, and Uncle Lowell and the three of them left town. They hopped in a boxcar aboard a freight train for destination unknown.

According to my dad, in those days the bridges were used for wagons and trains. Well, as it happens, my grandpa was crying and hungry so they decided to jump off at a river bridge where the train had stopped for a wagon on the tracks just south of St. Paul, Nebraska. (The bridge is still there. I just saw it in 2007 when I flew in to give the eulogy for Uncle Charlie's son, Billy Andersen. He was a World War II veteran, serving on the same PT boats John F. Kennedy served on in the South Pacific.)

The Andersen Dairy

As the boys ventured into the woods by the North Loop River, they now had to survive and find a way to live. They ended up digging a *dugout*, as they called it, and that was now home. They hunted and fished for their food. Amazing story to me to this day...and as you might have gathered, I definitely did not come from money—but quite an interesting past.

As the boys continued to live off the land outside St. Paul, Nebraska, Grandpa Andersen slipped out of a cottonwood tree and broke his hip one day. There was a family in town by the name of Dixon. Their hearts went out to the boys when they saw him limp around town without medical care so they took them into their home. That was an extremely selfless gesture. That move may have saved my grandpa's life.

Uncle Charlie ended up doing odd jobs around town, saving as much money as he could. One of his jobs was working at the Meade's family dairy. They milked the cows at 3:00 AM and put the fresh milk into clean milk bottles for distribution in town...no homogenizing or whatever the process is today. It was real whole milk. Eventually Uncle Charlie saved enough money to purchase the dairy and that became the Andersen family's primary income.

The dairy operation extended into the Great Depression of the 1930s. The people of St. Paul didn't have much money due to the high unemployment rate. But the Andersen Dairy continued to deliver the milk, and made sure all the kids had milk, even if the family could not afford to pay. My dad said that many families probably still owe money to Uncle Charlie and the Andersen family. At the time, it was the right thing to do, even though money was tight for Uncle Charlie and Grandpa Andersen.

Eventually my grandpa got a job building bridges with the Union Pacific railroad and bought a small eight-hundred-square-foot home for a few hundred dollars. My father and his two sisters were born in that four-room home. In time, my great-grandpa, Peter Andersen, found the boys and they forgave him for his past. He moved to St. Paul and died in that little house around 1925.

I felt compelled to tell that story because it is an amazing tale of how the Andersen family started in America and it has never been recorded. Most of them have passed and my aging dad pieced it together as best he could. Unfortunately, the boys' older brother, Lawrence, or Uncle Lowell, as he was called by my dad and his sisters, ended up dying in St. Paul of influenza at age twenty-eight.

Another amazing story about the character of Grandpa Andersen was recorded in a Grand Island, Nebraska, newspaper around 1950. He had to retire from the railroad because of a bad heart and started selling minnows for bait to fishermen that passed by their small home on Highway 281 in St. Paul. He would walk to the North Loop River and seine the minnows. (He ended up dying of a heart attack in that river on May 18, 1962.) His income consisted of a railroad pension, his small bait business, and a Veterans' Administration disability check he received for being wounded in World War I. He was wounded by shrapnel three days after the ceasefire because it took several days back then to get word to the front due to poor communication. My grandpa told the VA to cancel his disability check because he didn't need it anymore. He said he had enough money and that America could use it for a needier cause. The VA was shocked and had never had anyone refuse a disability check. Boy, could we use some of that character and philosophy in America now.

I am not ashamed to admit no member in my family has passed to the next world _and left behind_ what anyone would call a substantial net worth. Nevertheless, as I mentioned in _Living Well…Making a Difference,_ "_net worth does not equal self-worth._" I am so proud of the character they exhibited and the courage my uncle Charlie had to hold the boys together and earn some money to establish the dairy that provided milk for the kids of St. Paul, Nebraska, during the Great Depression.

It was the right thing to do and I'm afraid a trait America is losing. We need more Uncle Charlies and Grandpa Bills now as America is facing the greatest crisis since the depression. Where have our heroes gone? I contend it is still in all of us…but the focus has changed. We have to get back to the basics: caring about each other and making a difference.

Thank you, Uncle Charlie and Grandpa Andersen…you got it right.

Living Well

"The Andersens never skimmed the cream off the top of the milk."

St. Paul, Nebraska, circa 1934

The Andersen Dairy

My Andersen Dairy Checklist
(What can you do above and beyond the norm to impact others?)

1. _____

2. _____

3. _____

4. _____

5. _____

Chapter XIX

Footprints

I've learned that leaving footprints that others will want to follow in life is a deep human need.

My parents live in a manufactured home community in Tavares, Florida. The community is beautifully maintained and has a wonderful, peaceful air about it. Maybe that's because it is filled with people enjoying the golden years of their life, their winter years, so to speak. They're making their last impressions, their last memories of who they were on this earth.

By now you know that I like things simple. I was never accused of being the sharpest knife in the kitchen. I find the more I simplify my life, the better things seem to get. The idea of this chapter came to me on a cold night as I stepped out of the shower and saw my wet footprint on the floor mat. A moment later, I was off the mat and there was a watery imprint of my past.

Another crystallized moment in time. I have had several and discussed some in a previous chapter on moments in time. Well, one evening a few years ago, I took a walk with Mom and Dad in their "'hood" and saw something I will never forget. They took me by a home that had burned down that week. The old man who lived inside did not make it. His last few moments were spent escaping a burning double-wide trailer, suffering from smoke inhalation in bare and injured feet. His bloody footprints were still there on his driveway. I was captivated by the mark of his last few moments of life; there lay his DNA imprint. His spirit had departed moments after that mark was made. I thought to myself, *What marks had his spirit left? What footprints had he left on his family, friends, and the people in his circle of influence?*

At funerals, you almost never hear a eulogist talking about the size of the deceased's bank accounts or square footage of the home. Rather, the eulogist speaks about the impact the person had on other lives, the words the departed spoke and the actions he took that left imprints on other lives. I have given six eulogies so far and the number seems to be increasing. I consider that speaking venue one of the most powerful opportunities to leave an impact on others and possibly change their mindset on life.

Most people at funerals are feeling a deep sorrow for the loss of the loved one whose decaying body or cremated ashes lie before them. His true self or spirit has departed the earthly bounds. But the crowd is not only thinking of the death of a loved one. They are often coming to grips with their own mortality. As the eulogist, I have everyone's undivided attention. I stress that the departed has no second chance to right any wrongs or make more of a difference. So what were the footprints they left behind? Do you want to follow them? Will it make your walk through life better?

In April of 1987, I had just finished a seven-month cruise on the carrier *John F. Kennedy* as a catapult officer. Had some fun but worked hard in a very dangerous environment. I launched many jets off those mighty catapults at 0 to 140 mph in two seconds. When I returned from the cruise, I promised Cindy a week in Cancun, Mexico. We decided to drive to Chicago to drop the kids off with relatives then fly out of O'Hare Airport for a much-deserved vacation for BOTH of us. (Military deployments are probably tougher on spouses.)

As our luck would have it, a freak blizzard hit the Midwest in early April and we ended up stranded in Ohio on Interstate 70 overnight. Thank God we had enough gas to stay warm. Some local people were kind enough to invite us into their home, but we declined since both of our kids had chicken pox and were still contagious. So we all sat in the car contemplating our fate. Brad was five years old at the time. I remember his comment as the weather worsened and our anxiety grew: "I thought vacation was going to be more fun than this."

Living Well

At some point during the late evening, we had exhausted our drinking supplies. I remember we had some beef jerky and crackers left but no water or soda. Then through the blowing snow I saw the glow of a red Coke machine at a nearby park off the road. I decided to make the trek through the two-foot snowdrifts and finally made it to the machine. As I put my coins in, to my surprise out came two Cokes for the price of one. *Must be my lucky day,* I thought…and what a great ad for Coke!

As I turned to make my return to the car and my snowbound family, I found my journey much easier because I followed *my footprints.* They were impressions that had already been made in uncertain terrain in a hostile environment. The trip back was much easier and less hazardous.

Isn't that what we want to do for others? Leave footprints that they will want to follow, that you have tried and learned from, making their journey through life easier. Lessons learned from the lives of loved ones and those who go before us.

Time is short. At the Naval Academy, plebes or freshmen have to make chow calls before a meal. They stand outside upperclassmen's rooms in the halls and shout out what the menu is for the upcoming meal. At the end of their call, before running to formation, the plebe says, "Time, tide, and formation wait for no man."

It's time to leave some life-changing footprints that others will want to follow.

Footprints

"The need for meaning is not a biological need... nor is it psychological; it is a religious need... the thirst of our souls."

Harold Kushner

What Foot Prints Do I Want to Leave Behind? Checklist

1. _____

2. _____

3. _____

4. _____

5. _____

Chapter XX

Closing

I have learned that life is short and passing on life's lessons to those "living messages [our children] of a future we will never see" is vital to the future joy of our family and friends for generations to come.

As I close this book, I am sitting in one of the most peaceful rooms I know. It's unofficially called the "couch room" on our church campus. It's very quiet and serene with some old, very worn, and comfortable couches in it. I hope they never get rid of these old rifle stocks. I sit here and reflect on the wonderful stories and tear-filled moments I've seen people spend in sharing their lives on these old couches. Sharing lessons learned, seated with comfort and peace. Sound familiar? I hope so.

Living Well

After a while in hospice, you can kind of tell how much time a person has left before their soul departs the body. As my friend Wilson approached eternity, his lungs were failing as his body systematically shut down, as it will for all of us one day. He had an oxygen machine with water in it and you could hear it as he took each breath and see the internal mechanism move up and down. As I watched him weaken, it hit me that he only had a few of those breaths left. It was another crystallized moment in time for me.

So what are you doing with your remaining time? I hope you are enjoying it but also enriching the lives of others.

The gist of my first book was the concept of the joy that comes to your own life when you care about others. I was trying to convey the same thing with this book but with a different angle: improving other lives by passing on your lessons in life…and we all have them.

In my experiences in the military flying aircraft, sailing on navy vessels, and sometimes carrying the bags for Secretary of Defense Cohen, I have seen roughly forty-five countries. One sleepless night I lay awake and counted the countries. I've travelled from one side of this planet to the other. One thing I noticed is people are all basically the same. They want the same things you want: good health, a loving family, a sense of purpose. I believe we all have an inner, deep desire to make a mark and do something that outlasts our life. Unfortunately, some people don't seem to get that last part 'til it's almost too late.

Closing

In my life, I have seen a lot of things: some good, some not so good. I've experienced deep pain and incredible joy. And yet when I look back, it seems to come together like a beautiful mosaic. I heard a speaker at my church named Mike Lawrence once say, "Life is like a beautiful mosaic, often made from several pieces of shattered, colored glass. Individually they look like a single piece of shattered, worthless glass, but when you put them together, they make a beautiful mosaic called life." I often feel my life has been like many pieces of shattered glass due to family issues, terrible decisions, poor conduct, bad circumstances, people with an agenda, bad habits, etc., etc. But when I look back at almost every juncture, the event, job loss, or person I met had significance and has spun itself into my life and put me where I am today. I believe God has a purpose for each of us.

You have to remember there will never be another you. Be yourself, go with the flow, and care about others. Pass on what you have learned in life. Leave some footprints others will want and need to follow. No one on earth has precisely the mission to which God has assigned you. There is no one else who can offer God's love to others in just the same way you can. Start now. Time is fleeting.

I heard a man on a talk-radio show mention a poem or story about a great chasm. A chasm is defined as a wide fissure, crevice, or gorge in the earth, something that would impede or stop your progress to your destination. As the story was paraphrased, it describes how a man has spent his entire life trying to reach a certain destination. Perhaps it was success (depending on how you define it), peace of mind, a million dollars, an authored book...whatever. But as he ages and is near the end of his life, he encounters a great chasm blocking his goal in life. He attempts to cross the chasm at various places where, metaphorically speaking, the current is too fast, the rocks too treacherous, or perhaps the river too deep. He almost loses his life at a couple places and wishes he had known a different path to another position that might have made the crossing easier—or, had he known, he would have brought the proper gear for the crossing. Or, as we say in the military, some "better intelligence information."

Finally, after several attempts, he successfully crosses the great chasm. His goal is in sight. But then he slowly turns back and thinks it would have been much easier had he only known. Instead of moving on, he begins to build a bridge over the easiest way to traverse the chasm. He spends the rest of his life building this bridge. As he nears the end of his life, another weary traveler asks why, after so much toil to traverse, he didn't proceed to his destination. The old man said he felt his time remaining would be more worthwhile in paving life's path for those he would leave behind.

I have definitely learned that life is not easy. Last night I had another one of those sleepless nights anticipating some future issues that have yet to arrive...wondering how I will cross the chasm. I'm still hoping for sage advice from those who have been there before; it's usually a blessing to me. Many of my life lessons have been extremely painful to venture alone, but could

Closing

have been much easier with a bridge or intel from those who have gone before me.

I hope and pray these few chapters have helped you with your future chasms and will inspire you to *Make a Difference* for those you leave behind. On your deathbed, you won't regret it and will understand the true essence of *Living Well*.

God's peace to you all...
Andy

"The great use of life is to spend it for something that outlasts it."

William James (1842-1910)

Brief Afterword

My first thought is to thank you again for taking your precious time to read this simple message in the face of the pace of life.

I believe we all have lessons learned in our life. I cannot believe there is a soul out there who hasn't said, "Boy, if I had only known that…" or, "I wish I would not have done that. What was I thinking?" Then why wouldn't we want to pass it on to others?

I guess many people don't care; they're just here for a few years then out of here. "So get all I can, can what I get, sit on the can…then the hell with the rest of the world." That is the mentality I tried to tackle in *Living Well…Making a Difference*: life is not about you.

So my goal was to pass on some of my lessons learned and thoughts that may spur some of your own lessons learned, perhaps improve your life, and thereby give you some incentive to improve others'.

Give it all you have got 'til that last gasp of air when you blossom from a caterpillar into a beautiful, heavenly butterfly.

Well, it's time to move on to *Living Well III*…hope to see you there.

Author Biography

Christy, Brad, Baby Evan, Cindy, Andy, Baby Shay, Stephanie, Matt, and Brady

Andy Andersen graduated from the US Naval Academy and later obtained his master's degree from the Naval War College. Among other assignments as a pilot, he commanded two squadrons, was a catapult officer on the *USS John F. Kennedy*, and served in the Pentagon as deputy executive secretary to the secretary of defense. He retired from the navy as a captain with twenty-four years of service. He has been a public speaker for years for both navy and civilian audiences. An active member of Mandarin Presbyterian Church and a hospice volunteer, he also enjoys golf, jogging, and ice hockey. He and his wife, Cindy, have two grown, married sons and three grandchildren, and live in St. Johns, Florida. This is his second book.

You can contact Andy for speaking engagements through his website, andyandersen.net. A significant portion of his honorariums are donated to a charitable cause or organization.

Works Cited

Everyone's Normal 'Till You Get to Know Them, John Ortberg, Zondervan Publishing, Grand Rapids, Michigan, 2003

Half Time, Bob Buford, Zondervan Publishing, Grand Rapids, Michigan, 2003

How to Want What You Have, Dr. Timothy Miller, Avon Books, New York, New York, 1995

Making Life Rich Without Any Money, Phil Callaway, Harvest House Publishing, Eugene, Oregon, 1998

Out Live Your Life: You Were Made to Make a Difference, Max Lucado, Thomas Nelson Publishing, Nashville, Tennessee, 2010

The Paradox of Choice, Why More Is Less, Barry Schwartz, Harper Collins Publishing, New York, New York, 2004

The Me I Want to Be, John Ortberg, Zondervan Publishing, Grand Rapids, Michigan, 2010

When All You've Ever Wanted Isn't Enough, Harold Kushner, Summit Books, New York, New York, 1986

Endnotes

Chapter 4—Moments in Time: Precious Present

1. Miller, Timothy, *How to Want What You Have* (New York, New York: Avon Books, 1995), 3

2. Ibid, 9

Chapter 5—Going with the Flow

1. Schwartz, Barry, *The Paradox of Choice: Why More Is Less* (New York, New York: Harper Collins Publishers, 2004), 4

Chapter 6—Slowing Down

1. Dr. Kenneth Greenspan, director of the Center for Stress-Related Disorders at New York's Presbyterian Hospital, reported by Rowland Croucher in *Stress and Burnout* (John Mark Ministries)

Chapter 7—From Success to Significance

1. Buford, Bob, *Half Time* (Grand Rapids, Michigan: Zondervan, 1994)

2. Kushner, Harold, *When All You've Ever Wanted Isn't Enough* (New York, New York: Summit Books, 1986)

3. Ibid

4. Lucado, Max, *Out Live Your Life* (Nashville, Tennessee: Thomas Nelson, 2010), 4

Chapter 14—Contentment

1. Philippians 4:10 (*New International Version Bible*)

Chapter 16—Be Who You Are

1. Ortberg, John, *The Me I Want to Be* (Grand Rapids, Michigan: Zondervan, 2010), 221

2. Ibid, 223

3. Romans 12:2, *New International Version Bible*

87398012R00093

Made in the USA
San Bernardino, CA
04 September 2018